Small Talk

MORE JAZZ CHANTS®

CAROLYN GRAHAM

OXFORD UNIVERSITY PRESS

Oxford University Press
200 Madison Avenue, New York, N.Y. 10016 USA

Walton Street Oxford OX2 6DP England

OXFORD is a trademark of Oxford University Press.

Library of Congress Cataloging-in-Publication Data

Graham, Carolyn.
  Small talk.

  1. English language—Text-books for foreign speakers. 2.
English language—Spoken English. 3. Chants. I. Title.
PE1128.G652   1986   428.3'4   86-2417

ISBN 0-19-434220-4

ISBN 0-19-434221-2 (cassettes)

Printing (last digit): 9 8 7

Printed in the United States of America.

Jazz Chants® is a registered trademark of Oxford University Press.

Contents

Unit 1

Unit 2

Unit 3

Unit 4

Acknowledgments

I would like to express my thanks to Margot Gramer, my editor at Oxford University Press, for her dedication and support.

I would also like to express particular thanks to Matt Kaplowitz, who served as arranger and musical director for the cassette recording, and to Dick Hyman, Milt Hinton, and Ron Traxler for their inspired performance.

New York City
1985

What Is a Jazz Chant?

A jazz chant is the rhythmic expression of standard American English as it occurs in a situational context. The jazz chants included in *Small Talk* and on its accompanying cassette are designed as a language tool to develop students' appreciation of the rhythm and intonation patterns of spoken American English.

Just as the selection of a particular tempo and beat in jazz may convey powerful and varied emotions, the rhythm, stress, and intonation patterns of the spoken language are essential elements for the expression of the feelings and intent of the speaker. Linking these two dynamic forms has produced an innovative and exciting approach to language learning.

In performing the chants, students are also learning to distinguish difficult vowel and consonant contrasts while they are actively engaged in a verbal exchange that can easily be used in their own lives.

The Sounds of American English

American English stretches, shortens, blends, and often drops sounds. These subtle features of the language are extremely difficult for a student to comprehend unless his ear has been properly trained to understand the language of an educated native speaker in natural conversation. The sound of "Jeet yet?" is meaningless unless one has acquired the listening comprehension skills necessary to make the connection with "Did you eat yet?" Another example of the blending of sounds is *I'm going to (go)*, reduced to *I'm gonna (go)*. Students should be aware that the written word *gonna* would be considered nonstandard English whereas the spoken form is perfectly acceptable in American conversation.

A comparison of the text of *Small Talk* and its cassette helps to illustrate this striking difference between the written word and its spoken form. Jazz chants are particularly useful in developing these listening comprehension skills.

Organization of *Small Talk*

Small Talk is arranged by functions, or "purposes" for using language. Each unit begins with a number of jazz chants related to a given function, for example, *Greetings*. Within the group of chants, there often is a progression from a formal to a less formal way of expressing the function. The text is accompanied by a cassette of the chants to provide a means of self-study. An asterisk at the end of the title of a chant indicates that it is repeated on the *Small Talk* cassette.

Following the chants are pronunciation and listening exercises related to the functional topic of the chapter. Once the class has practiced and performed the chants, they can receive additional reinforcement through these exercises.

An answer key in the back of the book allows students to work at their own pace or individually. So, too, all of the listening exercises have been recorded on a separate cassette for that purpose.

Presenting the Chants

Jazz chants are based on a combination of repetition and learned response. The essential element in presenting a chant is to maintain a clear, steady beat and rhythm.

Initially, the students should repeat the lines of the chant following a model provided by the teacher and/or the cassette. Once the students are familiar with the material, they should progress from a simple choral repetition of a phrase to giving a group response in answer to a question or statement. This introduces an important new element as the class is now engaged in a dialogue with the teacher. This dialogue may then be transformed into a three or four-part exchange.

Many of the chants lend themselves to role playing, which enables the students to move from the formal structure of the chants to an informal classroom improvisation, using what they have learned in a situational context. These improvisations give the students not only the opportunity to speak individually but to make choices of attitude in their responses. During the role playing, it is important to make sure that the students retain the rhythm and intonation patterns established earlier.

General Suggestions for Presenting the Chants

STEP 1   Explain the functional context of the chant, using either the students' native language or very simple English. You should clearly explain any vocabulary items or expressions which might present difficulties, and may wish to discuss the cultural implications of the material.

STEP 2   Have the students listen to the first presentation of the chant on the cassette or as read by you.

STEP 3   Have the students repeat any difficult sounds or particularly new or difficult structures.

STEP 4   Have the students repeat each line of the chant after you. It is important to establish a clear, strong beat by counting, clapping, using rhythm sticks, or snapping your fingers.

STEP 5   Have the students listen again to the solo presentation of the chant.

STEP 6   Divide the class into two (or three) groups, each taking a role in the dialogue of the chant. Have each group repeat their lines after you.

STEP 7   Have the students respond to you, taking one of the roles in the dialogue of the chant, without hearing you model it first.

STEP 8   Divide the class again and have them perform the chant without your model. You now serve as a conductor, keeping a solid, unifying beat while bringing in the two sections at the correct time.

STEP 9   Have the class continue to work with the chant by using three or four-part exchanges, pair work, and role playing.

Small Talk

MORE JAZZ CHANTS®

1 _____ Greetings

Notes

1. Hi! How Are You?
This chant offers practice in shifting the stress from **are** in the first speaker's greeting to **you** in the answering voice.

2. How's Jack?
Students practice the subject pronouns in contraction with *is*, *am*, and *are*. It is important that students be able to recognize the masculine and feminine names in order to practice this chant correctly. This chant also offers an example of a typical response to bad news, *Oh no!*

1 Hi! How Are You? ★
(a casual greeting)

Hi! How *are* you?
      Fine. How are *you*?
Hi! How *are* you?
      Fine. How are *you*?

Hi! How *are* you?
Hi! How *are* you?
Hi! How *are* you?
      Fine. How are *you*?

2 How's Jack? ★
(greeting someone and asking about mutual friends)

Hi! How *are* you?
      Fine. How are *you*?
I'm fine. How's Bill?
      He's fine.
How's Mary?
      She's fine.
How are the children?
      They're fine.
How's your job?
      It's fine.
How's Jack?
      He's sick!
Oh no!

3. Hello. How've You Been?
Students practice the sound of the contractions *it's* and *how've*. This chant offers practice in shifting the stress from *It's **so** good to see you* to *It's good to see **you***.

3 Hello. How've You Been? ★
(greeting someone you haven't seen in a long time)

Hello. How've you been?
It's *so* good to see you.
        It's good to see *you*.
        How've you been?
Just fine.

Hello, how've you been?
Hello, how've you been?
Hello, how've you been?
        Just fine.
        Just fine.
It's *so* good to see you.
It's *so* good to see you.
        It's good to see *you*.
        How've you *been*?
Just fine.

4. Hello? Hello?
Students practice the rising intonation of *hello* used in answering the telephone. This chant also offers practice in the intonation pattern used to seek clarification of the last name, *Bill **who**?*

4 Hello? Hello? ★
(an informal greeting on the telephone)

Hello? Hello?
        Hi, Sue, this is Bill.
Bill? Bill *who*?
        Bill Brown.
Oh hi! How are *you*?

5. Jack! You're Back!
This chant offers practice in the sound of the contractions *you're*, *haven't*, *how've*, *it's*, and *I'm*. Students should also note the reduction in the sound of *am* in *So am I*.

5 Jack! You're Back! ★

(greeting a friend who has been away)

Jack! You're back!
I haven't seen you for a long time.
How've you been?
　　　　Just fine.
　　　　It's been a long time.
How've you been?
　　　　Just fine.
　　　　It's been a long time.

I'm so glad you're back, Jack.
　　　　So am I.
I'm so glad you're back, Jack.
　　　　So am I.
I'm so glad you're back.
I'm so glad you're back.
I'm so glad you're back, Jack.
　　　　So am I.
I haven't seen you for a long time.

Unit 1 Exercises

Exercise 1

Listen carefully as your teacher reads the sentences. Then listen again as your teacher repeats them. Fill in the blanks with the correct words. Check your answers in the Appendix.

1. _____ Mary. _____ _____ mother?

2. _____ fine, thank you. _____ Bill?

3. _____ fine. _____ _____ _____ children?

4. _____ fine. _____ _____ job?

5. _____ fine. _____ _____ good _____ see _____ .

6. _____ good _____ _____ you.

7. _____ _____ glad _____ back.

8. _____ _____ I. I _____ _____ you _____ _____ long _____ .

Exercise 2

Listen carefully while your teacher reads the sentences. Write them in the blanks below. Note the suggestions for careful listening. Check your answers in the Appendix.

1. _____ (three words)
   Listen for the sound of the contraction and the reduced vowel sound in *your*.

2. _____ (six words)
   Listen for the sound of the contraction and the reduced vowel sound in *to*.

3. _____ (three words)
   Listen for the sound of the contraction.

4. _____ (eight words)
   Listen for the sound of the contraction and the reduced vowel sound in *for*.

5. _____ (five words)
   Listen for the sound of the contraction and the reduced vowel sound in *you're*.

Exercise 3

Practice this dialogue with a partner.

- ■ Yes?
- □ Hello?
- ■ I'm sorry. I can't hear you very well. Who is this?
- □ It's your mother.
- ■ Oh, hi, Mom. How are you?
- □ I'm all right. How are *you*? You sound tired.
- ■ Oh no, I'm just fine. How's Dad?
- □ He's fine. How are your classes?
- ■ They're OK. How's everything at home?
- □ Just fine. Are you sure you don't have a cold?
- ■ No, no, I'm fine.
- □ Take some aspirin.
- ■ Mom, I told you. I don't have a cold.
- □ Call me when you're feeling better.
- ■ OK, Mom.

2 — Introductions/Identifying Self and Others

Notes

1. Harry, This Is Mary

This chant offers practice in a casual and frequently used form to introduce friends. The first variation presents the familiar *How do you do?* Students should be reminded that *How do you do?* is not meant as a question but is an example of ritual language, answered by the identical *How do you do?* The second variation offers practice in the contraction *I'd* and the shifting stress pattern in *I'm very glad to **meet** you/**Thank** you, I'm glad to meet **you**.*

2. Nice to Meet You

This chant offers practice in a short form of introduction which drops the *it's*, as in *It's nice to meet you*. Students should be reminded of the shifting stress pattern in ***Nice** to meet you/Nice to meet **you**.*

1 Harry, This Is Mary ★
(an informal introduction)

Harry, this is Mary.
    Hi.
        Hello.

(a more formal variation)

Harry, this is Mary.
    How do you do?
        How do you do?

(a formal variation)

Harry, I'd like you to meet my sister Mary.
    How do you do, Mary.
    I'm very glad to *meet* you.
        Thank you, I'm glad to meet *you*.

2 Nice to Meet You ★

Nice to meet you.
    Nice to meet *you*.
Nice to meet you.
    Nice to meet *you*.
Nice to meet you.
I'm *so* glad to meet you.
    Thank you, I'm glad to meet *you*.

3. I'm Glad to Meet You. I've Heard So Much About You
This chant offers practice in the contractions *I'm* and *I've* and illustrates the use of *much* and *many*. Students should pay special attention to the sound of the plural *s* in *things* and the shifting stress pattern *I've heard so much about you/Thank you, I'm glad to meet you.*

3 I'm Glad to Meet You. I've Heard So Much About You

I'm glad to meet you.
I've heard so much about you.
I'm glad to meet you.
I've heard so much about you.
I'm glad to meet you.
I've heard so much about you.
> Thank you, I'm glad to meet *you.*

I've heard so many nice things about you.
I've heard so many nice things about you.
So many nice things.
I've heard so many nice things.
I've heard so many nice things about you.
I'm glad to meet you.
I've heard so much about you.
> Thank you, I'm glad to meet *you.*

4. What's Your Name? Where Are You From?
This chant offers students practice in the sound and rhythm of these high frequency information questions. Students should practice the vowel reductions in *what's your* (what's-yer) and *where are* (where-er). Extend chant to include other forms (What's his/her name, where is he/she from?).

4 What's Your Name? Where Are You From?

What's your name?
Where are you from?
What's your name?
Where are you from?
What's your name?
Where are you from?
How long have you been here?

How long have you been here?
How long have you been here?
What's your name?
Where are you from?
How long have you been here?

8

5. What's Your First Name? How Do You Spell It?

This chant offers practice in the pronunciation of individual letters of the alphabet and in the two important information questions, *How do you spell it?*/*How do you pronounce it?* It can be used as a useful in-class exercise during the first days of class when students are getting to know each other.

5 What's Your First Name? How Do You Spell It?

What's your first name?
    Mary.
How do you spell it?
    M–A–R–Y.
    M.
M.
    A.
A.
    R.
R.
    Y.
Y.
M–A–R–Y. M–A–R–Y.

How do you pronounce it?
    Mary.
How do you spell it?
    M–A–R–Y.
How do you pronounce it?
    Mary.

Unit 2 Exercises

Exercise 1

Listen carefully as your teacher reads the sentences. Then listen again as your teacher repeats them. Fill in the blanks with the correct words. Check your answers in the Appendix.

1. Harry, _____ like _____ _____ meet _____ sister Mary.

2. How _____ _____ _____, Mary. _____ very _____ _____ meet _____ .

3. _____ you. _____ glad _____ _____ you. _____ heard _____ much _____ you.

4. How _____ _____ you _____ here?

5. _____ been _____ for _____ long _____ .

6. Bill, _____ like _____ _____ meet _____ friend Jane.

7. _____, Jane. _____ heard _____ many _____ _____ about _____ .

8. Thank you. Where _____ _____ _____ ?

9. _____ _____ New York.

10. _____ _____ I.

Exercise 2

Practice the following exchanges with a partner.

■ I'm *so* glad to see you.
□ It's wonderful to see *you*.

■ You look great.
□ So do you.

■ It was nice *meeting* you.
□ It was nice meeting *you*.

■ I'd like to meet him.
□ So would I.

■ I've never met him.
□ Neither have I.

■ I'm looking forward to meeting them.
□ So am I.

■ Haven't I met you somewhere before?
□ I don't think so.

Exercise 3

Listen carefully while your teacher reads the sentences. Write them in the blanks below. Note the suggestions for careful listening. Check your answers in the Appendix.

1. _____ (eight words)
   Listen for the sound of the contraction and the plural *s*.

2. _____ (six words)
   Listen for the reduced vowel sound in *have*.

3. _____ (six words)
   Listen for the sound of the contraction and the reduced vowel sound in *to*.

4. _____ (seven words)
   Listen for the reduced vowel sounds in *do/your*.

5. _____ (five words)
   Listen for the reduced vowel sounds in *do/it*.

3   Saying Good-bye

Notes

1. Good-bye, Good-bye

This chant offers three simple forms of saying good-bye: *good-bye/bye-bye/so long*. Students should note that *See you tomorrow* is the shortened version of "I'll see you . . . ."

2. Have a Nice Weekend

This chant offers practice in the high frequency expressions *Have a nice weekend/Have fun.* You might wish to include "Have a good day." Students should pay special attention to the pronunciation of the final *s* in *thanks*.

1 Good-bye, Good-bye
(*a casual good-bye to a friend*)

Good-bye, good-bye.
See you tomorrow.
     Bye-bye.

Good-bye, see you tomorrow.
Good-bye, see you tomorrow.
     Bye-bye.
     See you tomorrow.
     Bye-bye.
     Bye-bye.

So long, see you tomorrow.
So long, see you tomorrow.
So long, see you tomorrow.
     Bye-bye.

2 Have a Nice Weekend

Have a nice weekend.
     Thanks, you too.
Have a nice weekend.
     Thanks, you too.
Have a nice weekend.
See you on Monday.
Have a nice weekend.
     Thanks, you too.
Have a nice weekend.
See you on Monday.
Have fun.
     Thanks, you too.

3 It's Getting Late

It's getting late.
It's getting late.
It's getting late,
and I really hate
to say good-bye.
        Please don't go.
It's getting late,
and I really hate
to say good-bye.
        Please don't go.
It's getting late.
        Please don't go.
It's getting late.
        Please don't go.
It's getting late.
        Please don't go.
I've got to go home.
        Please don't go.
It's getting late,
and I really hate
to say good-bye,
but I've got to go home.
        Oh no, please don't go.
        Oh no, please don't go.
I've got to go home.
        Oh no, please don't go.
        Oh no, please don't go.

4 It Was Nice Seeing You Again

It was nice *seeing* you again.
        Thanks.
        It was nice seeing *you*.

I enjoyed *seeing* you again.
        Thanks.
        I enjoyed seeing *you*.

It was *so* nice.
        I enjoyed it too.
It was *so* nice.
        I enjoyed it too.
It was nice *seeing* you.
        Thanks.
        It was nice seeing *you*.

5 Good-bye, Harry, Say Hello to Mary

Good-bye, Harry, say hello to Mary.
   I will.
    Say hello to Bill.

Bye-bye, Jack, say hello to Jill.
Tell her I miss her.
   I will.

So long, Mary, say hello to Harry.
Tell him I miss him.
   I will.

6 We're Going to Miss You

We're going to miss you.
We *really* are.
We're going to miss you.
We *really* are.
We're *really* going to miss you.
We're *really* going to miss you.
   I'm going to miss you too.
   I'm going to miss you too.
   I'm *really* going to miss you.

We're going to miss you.
We *really* are.
   I'm going to miss you too.
   I *really* am.
We're going to miss you.
We *really* are.
   I'm going to miss you too.
   I *really* am.

Unit 3 Exercises

Exercise 1

Listen carefully as your teacher reads the sentences. Then listen again as your teacher repeats them. Fill in the blanks with the correct words. Check your answers in the Appendix.

1. _____ . _____ you _____ .

2. _____ long. Have _____ nice _____ .

3. _____ _____ late and _____ got

    _____ _____ home.

4. I _____ hate _____ _____ good-bye.

5. It _____ nice _____ you _____ .

6. _____ hello _____ Jack. Tell _____

    I miss _____ .

7. Say _____ _____ Mary. _____ _____

    I _____ _____ .

8. _____ going _____ miss you. We _____ are.

9. _____ _____ _____ miss

    _____ _____ . I _____ am.

10. Please _____ go. I'm _____ going

    _____ _____ you.

Exercise 2

Listen carefully while your teacher reads the sentences. Write them in the blanks below. Note the suggestions for careful listening. Check your answers in the Appendix.

1. _____ (five words)
   Listen for the sound of the contraction and the reduced vowel sound in *to*.

2. _____ (five words)
   Listen for the disappearing *h* in *him*.

3. _____ (six words)
   Listen for the disappearing *h* in *hello* and the reduced vowel sound in *to*.

4. _____ (five words)
   Listen for the sound of the contraction and the reduced vowel sound in *going to*.

5. _____ (five words)
   Listen for the reduced vowel sound in *was*.

Exercise 3

Listen as your teacher reads you the clues to the word puzzle. Write the words in the blanks after each number. Check your answers in the Appendix.

1.   G   ___ ___ ___

2.   O   ___ ___

3.   ___ ___ O

4. ___ ___ ___ D

5.   B   ___ ___ ___

6.   Y   ___ ___ ___ ___ ___

7.   E   ___ ___

4 Giving and Receiving Compliments

Notes

1. You Look Wonderful Today
This chant offers practice in the sound of the reduced vowels in *today*, *so*, and *do*, the sound of the contractions *that's* and *I'm*, and the plural *s* in *thanks*.

1 You Look Wonderful Today ★

You look wonderful today.
　　　So do you.
You look wonderful today.
　　　So do you.
That's a nice color on you.
　　　Thanks a lot.
That's a nice color on you.
　　　Thanks a lot.
　　　I'm glad you like it.
That's a wonderful color on you.
　　　Thanks a lot.
　　　I'm very glad you like it.

2. That's a Nice Sweater
This chant includes examples of the contracted forms *that's*, *it's*, *I'm*, and *they're* and practice in the sound of *it*, *them*, and *those are*.

2 That's a Nice Sweater ★

That's a nice sweater.
Is it new?
　　　Yes, it is.
Where did you get it?
　　　I got it at Macy's.
It's beautiful.
　　　Thank you.
　　　I'm glad you like it.

Those are nice boots.
Are they new?
　　　Yes, they are.
Where did you get them?
　　　I got them at Macy's.
They're beautiful.
　　　Thank you.
　　　I'm glad you like them.

3. **I Like Your Gloves**
This chant offers practice in the sound of the contractions *I've*, *they're*, and *it's*. Students should note the sound of *it* and *them*.

3 I Like Your Gloves ★

I like your gloves.
Are they new?
   Oh no. I've had them for years.
Where did you get them?
   I got them in London.
They're beautiful.
   Thank you.

I like your ring.
Is it new?
   Oh no. I've had it for years.
Where did you get it?
   I got it in India.
It's beautiful.
   Thank you.

4. **You Look Marvelous! You Haven't Changed a Bit**
This chant provides practice in the sound of the contraction *haven't* and the reduced vowel sounds in *so*, *do*, and *have*. It also offers practice in the use of *So do you/Neither have you*.

4 You Look Marvelous! You Haven't Changed a Bit ★

(complimenting a person you haven't seen for a long time)

You look marvelous!
You haven't changed a bit.
   Neither have you.
   Neither have you.
You look marvelous!
   So do you.
You look wonderful!
   So do you.
You look terrific!
   So do you.
You haven't changed a bit.
   Neither have you.

5 You Speak English Very Well ★

You speak English very well.
> Oh no, not really.
Yes, you do, you really do.
> No, I don't.
Yes, you do.
> No, I don't.
Yes, you do.
> No, I don't.
> That's not true.
Yes, it is.
You really do speak English very well.
> Thank you.
> You're very kind.
No, I mean it.
I really mean it.
> Thank you.
> You're very kind.
No, I mean it.
I really mean it.
You really do speak English very well.
> Thank you.

6 I'm Afraid My English Is Not Very Good ★
(fishing for a compliment)

I'm afraid my English is not very good.
> Don't be silly.
> It's wonderful.
I'm afraid my English is not very good.
> Don't be silly.
> It's wonderful.
It's terrible.
> Don't be silly.
It's terrible.
> Don't be silly.
I'm afraid my English is not very good.
> Don't be silly.
> It's wonderful.

19

Unit 4 Exercises

Exercise 1

Listen carefully as your teacher reads the sentences. Then listen again as your teacher repeats them. Fill in the blanks with the correct words. Check your answers in the Appendix.

1. You ＿＿＿＿＿ wonderful ＿＿＿＿＿ .

2. Thanks, ＿＿＿＿＿ ＿＿＿＿＿ you.

3. ＿＿＿＿＿ ＿＿＿＿＿ nice ＿＿＿＿＿ on ＿＿＿＿＿ .

4. ＿＿＿＿＿ glad ＿＿＿＿＿ like ＿＿＿＿＿ .

5. ＿＿＿＿＿ ＿＿＿＿＿ nice ＿＿＿＿＿ .

   Is ＿＿＿＿＿ new?

6. Oh no. ＿＿＿＿＿ had ＿＿＿＿＿ ＿＿＿＿＿ years.

7. ＿＿＿＿＿ beautiful.

8. You ＿＿＿＿＿ changed ＿＿＿＿＿ ＿＿＿＿＿ .

9. I ＿＿＿＿＿ ＿＿＿＿＿ gloves. Are ＿＿＿＿＿ new?

10. Yes, ＿＿＿＿＿ are. I ＿＿＿＿＿ ＿＿＿＿＿

    ＿＿＿＿＿ Macy's.

Exercise 2

Listen carefully while your teacher reads the sentences. Write them in the blanks below. Note the suggestions for careful listening. Check your answers in the Appendix.

1. ＿＿＿＿＿＿＿＿＿＿＿＿＿＿＿＿＿＿＿ (four words)
   Listen for the sound of the contraction.

2. ＿＿＿＿＿＿＿＿＿＿＿＿＿＿＿＿＿＿＿ (five words)

3. ＿＿＿＿＿＿＿＿＿＿＿＿＿＿＿＿＿＿＿ (five words)

4. ＿＿＿＿＿＿＿＿＿＿＿＿＿＿＿＿＿＿＿ (six words)
   Listen for the sound of the contraction and the indefinite article *a*.

5. ＿＿＿＿＿＿＿＿＿＿＿＿＿＿＿＿＿＿＿ (four words)
   Listen for the sound of the plural *s*.

20

6. _____ (five words)

7. _____ (five words)

8. _____ (two words)

9. _____ (three words)

Listen for the sound of the plural *s*.

10. _____ (five words)

Exercise 3

Listen as your teacher reads you the clues to the word puzzle. Write the words in the blanks after each number. Check your answers in the Appendix.

1.   **G**   ___ ___ ___ ___

2.   **R**   ___ ___

3. ___ ___ ___ ___ **E**

4.   ___ ___ ___ **E**

5. ___ ___ ___ ___ **N**

Exercise 4

Practice this dialogue with a partner.

■ Well, what do you think?
□ About what?
■ My hat. Do you like it?
□ It's fine.
■ Is that all you have to say?
□ What do you want me to say? I said it's fine.
■ Do you like it?
□ Of course I like it.
■ I mean do you *really* like it?
□ I like it. I love it. I'm crazy about it. It's fabulous!
■ You don't have to overdo it.

5   Inviting/Accepting/Refusing

Notes

1. Let's Have Lunch
This chant offers practice in the contraction *let's* and the reduced vowel sounds in *today* and *tonight*.

1   Let's Have Lunch
(*a casual invitation*)

Let's have lunch today.
       OK.
Let's have lunch today.
       OK.
           Let's have lunch.
           Let's have lunch.
Let's have lunch today.
       OK.

Let's have dinner tonight.
       All right.
Let's have dinner tonight.
       All right.
Let's have dinner.
Let's have dinner.
Let's have dinner tonight.
       All right.

2. You Call Me or I'll Call You
Students practice the contractions *I'll, let's, when's,* and *I'm* and the reduced vowel sounds in *or, together,* and *to.*

2   You Call Me or I'll Call You
(*making indefinite plans to meet*)

You call me or I'll call you.
You call me or I'll call you.
Let's have lunch together someday.
       OK.
       I'll call you.

You call me.
You call me.
You call me or I'll call you.

You call me.
You call me.
You call me or I'll call you.

       When's the best time to call you?
       When's the best time to call you?
I'm usually home after seven.
I'm usually home after seven.
       When's the best time to call you?
I'm usually home after seven.

This chant offers practice in the contraction *I'd* and the reduced vowel sounds in *for, tonight,* and *should.* It also provides an example of a polite refusal: *I wish I could but I'm afraid I can't.*

3 Can You Come Over?

Can you come over for dinner tonight?
> I'd like that very much.

Can you come over for dinner tonight?
> I'd like that very much.
> What time should I come?
> What time should I come?

Come around six if you can.
> Fine.

Come around six if you can.
> Fine.

Can you come over?
Can you come over?
Can you come over for a drink tonight?
> I'd love to.
> I'd love to.

Can you come over for a drink tonight?
> I'd love to.

Can you come over for lunch tomorrow?
> I wish I could but I'm afraid I can't.

Oh, I'm sorry. That's too bad.
> I really wish I could.

4 We're Having a Party

We're having a party next Saturday night.
Can you come? Can you come?
> I'd love to.
> I'd love to.
> That sounds great.
> I'd love to.

We're having a party next Saturday night.
Can you come?
> I'd love to.
We're having a party.
I hope you can come.
> That sounds nice.
> I'd love to.
> Sounds great.
> Sounds good.
> Sounds like fun.
> I'd love to.

We're having a party next Saturday night.
Can you come? Can you come?
> I'd love to.
> I'd love to.
> That sounds great.
> I'd love to.

5 Would You Like to Go to the Movies Tonight?

Would you like to go to the movies tonight?
> I'd love to.
> I'd love to.
I feel like going to the movies tonight.
> I do too.
> Let's go.
I feel like going to the movies tonight.
> So do I.
> Let's go.
I don't feel like studying tonight.
> Neither do I.
> Let's go.

Unit 5 Exercises

Exercise 1

Listen carefully as your teacher reads the sentences. Then listen again as your teacher repeats them. Fill in the blanks with the correct words. Check your answers in the Appendix.

1. _____ _____ lunch _____ .

2. _____ _____ come _____ _____
   _____ drink _____ ?

3. _____ love _____ . _____ time
   _____ I _____ ?

4. _____ having _____ party _____ Saturday
   _____ . I _____ _____ can _____ .

5. I _____ I _____ but I'm _____ I _____ .

6. _____ _____ best _____ _____
   call _____ ?

7. I'm _____ home _____ seven.

8. You _____ me _____ _____
   call _____ .

9. I _____ like _____ _____ _____
   movies _____ .

10. I _____ _____ . _____ go.

Exercise 2

Choose a partner. Practice inviting, accepting, and refusing. The first speaker will choose one of the invitations and the second speaker will select any of the responses. Look at the example.

Example

Student A: Let's go out for pizza!
Student B: I'd love to.

Invitations

Do you feel like going to the movies tonight?
Let's go out for pizza!
Let's have coffee after class today.
Let's have lunch together sometime.
Can you come over for dinner tomorrow night?
We're going for a walk. Do you want to come with us?
Let's have dinner together tonight.
Let's get together for a drink some night.
Would you like to study English with me tonight?
Would you like to go to the movies this afternoon?

Responses

I'd love to.
That sounds nice.
I'd like that very much.
That's a wonderful idea.

Oh, I'm sorry, I'm busy.
I wish I could but I'm afraid I can't.
I'm sorry I can't. Maybe some other time.

Exercise 3

Practice this dialogue with a partner. Notice the strong and regular rhythmic pattern in each line.

- Would you like to have lunch with me tomorrow?
- I'm sorry, I can't. I'm busy tomorrow.
- How about Thursday?
- I can't do it on Thursday. What about Friday?
- I'm busy Friday. What about next Tuesday?
- Tuesday is impossible. What about Wednesday?
- I can't make it on Wednesday. What about Sunday?
- Sundays aren't too good for me. What about Monday?
- Monday is no good. What about a week from Wednesday?
- That sounds fine.

Exercise 4

Listen as your teacher reads you the clues to the word puzzle. Write the words in the blanks after each number. Check your answers in the Appendix.

1. P ___ ___ ___ ___ ___

2. A ___ ___ ___ ___

3. R ___ ___ ___ ___

4. T ___ ___ ___ ___

5. Y ___ ___ ___ ___ ___ ___ ___ ___

6 Expressing Likes and Dislikes
Asking For and Giving an Opinion

Notes

1. I Like It a Lot
This chant provides practice in the
sound of the reduced vowel in *it* and
the use of the emphatic forms *a lot/
very much/really.*

1 I Like It a Lot ★

I like it.
I like it a lot.
I love it.

I like it.
I like it a lot.
I love it.

I like it very much.
I like it very much.
I like it.
I like it a lot.
I love it.

I really like it very much.
I really like it very much.
I like it.
I like it a lot.
I love it.

2. Do You Like It?
This chant offers practice in the emphatic forms *really/a lot*, the reduced vowel sound in *it*, and the contraction *I'm*.

2 Do You Like It? ★

Do you like it?
        I like it a lot.
I'm glad.

Do you like it?
        I like it a lot.
I'm glad.

Do you like it?
Do you really like it?

Do you like it?
Do you really like it?

Do you like it?
Do you really like it?
        I like it a lot.
I'm glad.

3. How Do You Like It?
This chant offers practice in asking for an opinion or approval. Students should practice the sound of the contractions *it's* and *I'm*.

3 How Do You Like It? ★

How do you like it?
        I love it.
How do you like it?
        I like it a lot.
How do you like it?
        I like it a lot.
        It's wonderful.
I'm glad you like it.

Is this OK?
        It's wonderful.
Is this all right?
        It's wonderful.
Is this OK?
        It's wonderful.
Good.
I'm glad you like it.

4 It's All Right, I Guess ★

(*an unenthusiastic agreement*)

Will this be OK?
       It's all right, I guess.
       I guess it's all right.
       It'll do.
Are you sure it's OK?
       It's all right, I guess.
       I guess it's all right.
       It'll do.
       It'll have to do.
       It'll have to do.
Are you sure it's OK?
       It'll do.

5 It's Not Quite Right ★

(*a polite rejection*)

Is this all right?
       Not quite.
Is this all right?
       Not quite.
Is this all right?
       Not quite.
       It's not quite right.
       I'm afraid it's not quite right.
       Not quite right.
       I'm afraid it's not quite right.
       Not quite right.
I'm sorry you feel that way.
I'm sorry you feel that way.
I'm awfully sorry you feel that way.
       It's not quite right.

6. I Don't Like It At All

This chant offers practice in the sound of the contractions *don't* and *can't*. Students should notice the way the sounds are linked together in *like it/hate it/stand it/like it at all/ like it a bit/Not a bit/Not at all.*

6 I Don't Like It At All

I don't like it.
I don't like it at all.
    I hate it.
      I can't stand it.
I don't like it.
I don't like it at all.
    I hate it.
      I can't stand it.
I don't like it a bit.
I don't like it at all.
    I hate it.
      I can't stand it.
Not a bit.
Not a bit.
I don't like it a bit.

Not at all.
Not at all.
I don't like it at all.
    I hate it.
      I can't stand it.
I hate it.
I hate it.
      I can't stand it.
I hate it.
I hate it.
      I can't stand it.
I hate it.
I hate it.
      I can't stand it.
I hate it.
I hate it.
      I can't stand it.
I don't like it at all.

Unit 6 Exercises

Exercise 1

Listen carefully as your teacher reads the sentences. Then listen again as your teacher repeats them. Fill in the blanks with the correct words. Check your answers in the Appendix.

1. I _____ _____ _____ lot.

2. _____ glad _____ like _____ .

3. _____ afraid _____ not _____ right.

4. I _____ like _____ very _____ .

5. _____ all _____ , I _____ .

6. Will _____ be _____ ?

7. _____ have _____ _____ .

8. Are _____ sure _____ OK?

9. I _____ stand _____ .

10. _____ sorry _____ feel _____ way.

Exercise 2

Listen carefully while your teacher reads the sentences. Write them in the blanks below. Note the suggestions for careful listening. Check your answers in the Appendix.

1. _____ (six words)

2. _____ (six words)
   Listen for the sound of the contractions.

3. _____ (six words)
   Listen for the sound of the contraction and the reduced vowel sounds.

4. _____ (four words)
   Listen for the sound of the contraction and the reduced vowel sound in *it*.

5. _____ (five words)
   Listen for the sound of the contraction.

Exercise 3

Listen as your teacher reads the following paragraphs. Listen for the important information to make sure you understand the situation. Then choose a partner and create your own conversation between 1) the brother and the sister-in-law 2) Bob and his boss 3) Sally and her husband. Look at the example.

1. My sister-in-law just bought a new house but she's not very happy with it. It's a lot smaller than the old one and not as comfortable. My brother thinks it's wonderful. In fact, he really loves it because it has a large yard and he likes to work in the garden.

Example

Brother: I love the house. Don't you love it? Isn't it terrific?
Sister-in-law: It's OK.
Brother: What do you mean OK? It's great.
Sister-in-law: It's all right, I guess.

2. Bob has just started a new job. He likes his boss a lot and he enjoys his work but there is one problem. He has to be in the office at 8 A.M. every day. He likes to stay up late at night, so it's very hard for him to wake up early. He hates to be late but he's just not a morning person. He may have to look for another job.

3. Sally loves dogs but she can't stand cats. Cats make her very nervous. They scratch and bite and they are not as friendly as dogs. She thinks dogs are more intelligent but her husband doesn't agree. He prefers cats. They have two cats and a big dog. Sally takes care of the dog and her husband takes care of the cats. The dog hates the cats and the cats hate the dog.

7 Expressing Ability or Inability to Do Something/Making Excuses/Giving Encouragement

Notes

1. I Can't Do It
This chant provides practice in the important sound contrast of *can/can't*, with particular attention to the vowel reduction of *can* when it occurs in the body of a sentence, as in *You can do it.* Students should note that the *can* in this case is unstressed and pronounced as /kn/.

1 I Can't Do It

I can't do it.
I can't do it.
     Yes, you can.
     Yes, you can.
I can't do it.
     Yes, you can.
     You can do it.
     You can do it.

I can't do it.
     Yes, you can.
     You can do it.
     You can do it.
No, I can't.
     Yes, you can.
No, I can't.
     Yes, you can.
I can't do it.
     Yes, you can.
     You can do it.
     You can do it.

2 I Give Up

I give up.
I can't do it.
        Don't give up.
        Try it again.
I give up.
I can't do it.
        Don't give up.
        Try it again.

I read it once.
I couldn't understand it.
        Don't give up.
        Read it again.
I read it twice.
I couldn't understand it.
        Don't give up.
        Read it again.
I read it three times.
I couldn't understand it.
        Don't give up.
        Read it again.

I give up.
I can't do it.
        Don't give up.
        Try it again.

3 If I Can Do It You Can Do It

Do you think I can do it?
        Of course you can.
        If I can do it
        you can do it too.

Do you think I can do it?
        Of course you can.
        If I can do it
        you can do it too.
        Believe me,
        it's not that hard.
        Believe me,
        it's not that hard.
        You can do it
        just as well as I can.
        If I can do it
        you can do it too.

4. Can You Speak English?
This chant provides examples of describing language ability from limited (*Not very well/Just a little/Not at all*) to proficient (*Of course she can/It's her native language*). Students should note the disappearing *h* in *his* or *her native language*.

4 Can You Speak English?

Can you speak English?
>Not very well.

Can you speak Spanish?
>Not very well.

Can you speak French?
>Just a little.

Can you speak Chinese?
>Not at all.

Can you understand French?
>Just a little.

Can you understand Spanish?
>More or less.

Can you understand Turkish?
>Not at all.

Can you understand your teacher?
>Most of the time.

Can she speak French?
>>Of course she can.
>>It's her native language.
>>She was born in France.

Can he speak Japanese?
>>Of course he can.
>>It's his native language.
>>He was born in Japan.

5. I'm Afraid I Won't Be Able to Go
This chant offers practice in the sound of the contractions *I'm, won't,* and *that's*. It provides examples of expressions of dismay, *Oh no, what a shame!/that's too bad* in response to the statement of inability, *I won't be able to . . . .* Students should note the pronunciation of *have to* (hafta), used in the excuse *I have to work tomorrow*.

5 I'm Afraid I Won't Be Able to Go

I'm afraid I won't be able to go.
I'm coming down with a cold.
>>Oh no, what a shame!
>>Oh no, what a shame!

I'm afraid I won't be able to go.
I'm coming down with a cold.

I'm afraid I won't be able to go.
I have to work tomorrow.
I'm afraid I won't be able to go.
I have to work tomorrow.
>>Oh no, that's too bad.
>>Oh no, that's too bad.

I'm afraid I won't be able to go.
I'm coming down with a cold.

6. Will I Ever Learn to Speak
   English?
This chant provides examples of the
language of encouragement in
response to an insecure first
speaker, *Will I ever learn?* Students
should practice the short responses
*Of course you will/Of course you
can/Of course you are.*

6 Will I Ever Learn to Speak English?

Will I ever learn to speak English?
        Of course you will.
        You're doing fine.
        You're getting better
        all the time.

Will I ever learn?
Will I ever learn?
        Of course you will.
Do you think I can do it?
        Of course you can.

Am I doing all right?
Am I doing all right?
        Of course you are.
        You're doing fine.
        You're getting better
        all the time.
        You're getting better
        every day.
        You're getting better
        all the time.
Will I ever learn?
Will I ever learn?
        Of course you will.
        You're doing fine.
        You're getting better
        all the time.

Unit 7 Exercises

Exercise 1

Listen carefully as your teacher reads the sentences. Then listen again as your teacher repeats them. Fill in the blanks with the correct words. Check your answers in the Appendix.

1. I _____ _____ . I _____ do _____ .

2. I _____ _____ once. I _____
   understand _____ .

3. _____ I _____ learn _____ speak English?

4. _____ course _____ will. _____ getting
   _____ all _____ time.

5. _____ give _____ . Try _____ again.

6. _____ I _____ all _____ ?

7. _____ course _____ _____ .
   _____ doing _____ .

8. Can _____ speak French?

9. _____ course _____ can. _____ _____
   native _____ .

10. She _____ born _____ France.

Exercise 2

Listen carefully while your teacher reads the sentences. Write them in the blanks below. Note the suggestions for careful listening. Check your answers in the Appendix.

1. _____
_____ (seven words; two sentences)
Listen for the contraction *can't* and the reduced vowel sound in *it*.

2. _____
_____ (six words; two sentences)

3. _____ (ten words)
Listen for the reduced vowel sounds in *can/as/it*.

4. _____ (six words)

5. _____ (six words)
Listen for the sound of the contraction.

Exercise 3

Listen carefully as your teacher reads sentences one to ten at normal speed. If you hear *can*, check the box under *Wonderful*. If you hear *can't*, check the box under *Oh, I'm sorry*. Remember that the sound of *can* is pronounced as /kn/ and is unstressed. The sound of *can't* receives a strong stress. The sentences appear in the Appendix.

	Wonderful.	Oh, I'm sorry.
1.	☐	☐
2.	☐	☐
3.	☐	☐
4.	☐	☐
5.	☐	☐
6.	☐	☐
7.	☐	☐
8.	☐	☐
9.	☐	☐
10.	☐	☐

8   Apologizing/Accepting an Apology

Notes

1. I'm Sorry. That's All Right
This chant offers practice in the sound of the contractions *I'm, that's* and *don't,* the sound of the reduced vowel in *it,* and the use of **really** for emphasis.

1   I'm Sorry. That's All Right

I'm sorry.
> That's all right.

I'm *so* sorry.
> That's all right.

I'm *terribly* sorry.
> That's all right.
> Don't worry about it.
> That's all right.

I'm sorry I'm late.
> That's all right.

I'm *really* sorry.
> Never mind.
> Don't worry about it.
> That's all right.
> Never mind.
> Don't worry about it.
> Never mind.
> Don't worry about it.

I'm *really* sorry.
> Never mind.
> Don't worry about it.
> That's all right.

40

2. Excuse Me. That's OK. Never Mind. No Problem
This chant offers examples of the frequent pattern of using multiple responses to the apologetic *Excuse me*. It also provides practice in the sound of the contractions *that's*, *I'm*, and *don't* and illustrates the use of *terribly* for emphasis.

3. It's All My Fault
This chant offers practice in the sound of the contractions *it's*, *shouldn't*, *doesn't*, and *I'm* and the reduced vowel sound in *it*. It also offers an example of language which removes feelings of guilt, *It's not your fault*.

2 Excuse Me. That's OK. Never Mind. No Problem

Excuse me.
> That's OK.

Pardon me.
> That's all right.

Please excuse me.
> That's OK.
> Never mind.
> No problem.

Pardon me.
It was *my* mistake.
> That's all right.
> Don't worry about it.

I'm terribly sorry.
> That's OK.
> Never mind.
> No problem.

3 It's All My Fault

It's all my fault.
It's all my fault.
I shouldn't have done it.
It's all my fault.
> It doesn't matter.
> It's not important.

I'm terribly sorry.
It's all my fault.
> Don't be silly.
> You couldn't help it.

I'm terribly sorry.
> It's not your fault.
> Don't be silly.
> You couldn't help it.

I'm terribly sorry.
> It's not your fault.

4 I'm Sorry I Did It. I Shouldn't Have Done It

I'm sorry I did it.
I shouldn't have done it.
I'm sorry I did it.
I shouldn't have done it.
>> It doesn't matter.
>> It really doesn't.
>> It doesn't matter.
>> Honestly.

I'm sorry I took it.
I shouldn't have taken it.
I'm sorry I wore it.
I shouldn't have worn it.
I'm sorry I wrote it.
I shouldn't have written it.
>> It doesn't matter.
>> Honestly.

I should have told you.
>> It doesn't matter.
I should have told you.
>> It doesn't matter.
I shouldn't have done it.
>> It doesn't matter.
>> It really doesn't.
>> Honestly.

5 I'm Afraid I Owe You an Apology

I'm afraid I owe you an apology.
>> What for?
>> What for?
I'm sorry about last night.
>> There's nothing to apologize for.

I'm very sorry.
I'm really sorry.
I'm awfully sorry.
I'm terribly sorry.
I'm afraid I owe you an apology.
>> There's nothing to apologize for.
I'm sorry about last night.
I'm sorry about last night.
>> There's really nothing to apologize for.
I'm sorry about last night.

Unit 8 Exercises

Exercise 1

Listen carefully as your teacher reads the sentences. Then listen again as your teacher repeats them. Fill in the blanks with the correct words. Check your answers in the Appendix.

1. I'm _____ sorry. It _____
   my _____ .

2. _____ all _____ . Don't _____
   about _____ .

3. _____ all _____ fault. I _____
   _____ done _____ .

4. _____ be _____ . You _____
   help _____ .

5. I _____ have _____ you.

6. It _____ matter. _____ , it _____ .

7. I'm _____ I _____ you _____ apology.

8. I'm _____ about _____ night.

9. Don't _____ silly. _____ nothing to
   _____ for.

10. Please _____ me. I _____ have _____ it.

Exercise 2

Listen carefully while your teacher reads the sentences. Write them in the blanks below. Note the suggestions for careful listening. Check your answers in the Appendix.

1. _____

   _____ (six words; two sentences)
   Listen for the contractions *that's/doesn't.*

2. _____ (four words)
   Listen for the contraction *don't* and the reduced vowel sound in *it.*

3. _____ (five words)
   Listen for the sound of *should have* or *shouldn't have* and the reduced vowel sound in *it.*

4. _____ (five words)
   Listen for the sound of *should have* or *shouldn't have.*

5. _____ (five words)
   Listen for the reduced vowel sound in *an.*

Exercise 3

Practice the following dialogues with a partner.

Dialogue A
- You're late again!
- I'm *awfully* sorry.
- This is the third time this week!
- I'm afraid I overslept.
- That's no excuse. This has to stop!
- I'm *really* sorry. It won't happen again.
- I certainly hope not.

Dialogue B
- Oh, I'm *terribly* sorry about last night.
- Sorry? What *for?*
- I forgot to return your call.
- Oh, that's all right. It wasn't important.
- Are you *sure?*
- Of course. Don't worry about it.
- I should have remembered.
- Forget it.
- You're not angry?
- Of *course* not.

9   Talking About Food

Notes

1. Chicken Soup
This chant provides an example of the reduction in the sound of *and* ('n) as it occurs in *rice and beans*. Students should note the sound of the plural *s* in *beans* and the sound of the contraction *I'd*. This chant also offers practice in the use of *a bowl of/a cup of*.

1   Chicken Soup

Chicken.
Chicken soup.
Chicken.
Chicken soup.
          Rice and beans.
          Rice and beans.
                Whole wheat toast.
I'd like a bowl of soup.
          Chicken soup.
I'd like a bowl of soup.
          Chicken soup.
I'd like a large bowl of chicken soup.
I'd like a large bowl of soup.

I'd like a cup of soup.
          Chicken soup.
I'd like a cup of soup.
          Chicken soup.
I'd like a large cup of soup.

2. What Are You Going to Have?
This chant offers practice in the sound of *going to* (gonna) and provides an example of shifting stress in *What are you going to have?/What are **you** going to have?* Students should note the sound of the third person *s* in *sounds* and the use of the contraction *I'll*.

2   What Are You Going to Have?
(getting ready to order in a restaurant)

What are you going to have?
          Chicken soup.
Mm mm. That sounds good.
What are you going to have?
          Chicken soup.
I think I'll have the same.
What are you going to have?
          Chicken soup.
          What are *you* going to have?
Chicken soup.
What are *you* going to have?
          Chicken soup.
I think I'll have the same.
Mm mm. That sounds good.
That sounds good.
That sounds good.
Chicken soup! That sounds good.
I think I'll have the same.

3 I'd Like a Sandwich

I'd like a sandwich.
I'd like a sandwich.
I'd like a tuna salad sandwich.
  Tuna salad.
  Tuna salad.
  Tuna salad sandwich.
  Whole wheat toast.
  Whole wheat toast.
I'd like a tuna salad sandwich on whole wheat toast.
  Whole wheat toast.
  Whole wheat toast.
I'd like a tuna salad sandwich on whole wheat toast.
I'd like a large bowl of chicken soup.
I'd like a large bowl of chicken soup.
I'd like a large bowl of chicken soup
and a tuna salad sandwich on whole wheat toast.

4 I Haven't Decided Yet

What are you going to have for lunch?
  I haven't *decided* yet.
   What are *you* going to have?
I haven't *decided* yet.

What are you going to drink?
  I haven't *decided* yet.
   What are *you* going to have?
I haven't *decided* yet.

What are you going to have for dessert?
  I haven't *decided* yet.
   What are *you* going to have?
I haven't *decided* yet.
I haven't *decided* yet.

5. Salt and Pepper

This chant offers practice in the reduction of sound in *and* ('n) as it occurs in *salt and pepper/bread and butter.* It also provides practice in the high frequency expression *please pass the . . . .*

5 Salt and Pepper

Salt and pepper.
Salt and pepper.
Please pass the pepper.
Please pass the salt.
Pass the salt and pepper, please.
Please pass the pepper.
Please pass the salt.

Salt and pepper.
Bread and butter.
Pass the bread and butter, please.
Please pass the bread.
Please pass the butter.
Please pass the pepper.
Please pass the salt.

Unit 9 Exercises

Exercise 1

Listen carefully as your teacher reads the sentences. Then listen again as your teacher repeats them. Fill in the blanks with the correct words. Check your answers in the Appendix.

1. I think _____ have _____ large _____

   _____ chicken soup _____ .

2. What _____ you _____ _____ have?

3. I think _____ have _____ same.

4. What _____ you _____ _____ drink?

5. I _____ decided _____ .

6. _____ like _____ tuna salad _____

   _____ whole _____ toast.

7. That _____ good.

8. Pass _____ bread _____ butter, _____ .

9. Please _____ _____ pepper, _____ pass

   _____ salt.

10. _____ like rice _____ _____ .

Exercise 2

Listen carefully while your teacher reads the sentences. Write them in the blanks below. Note the suggestions for careful listening. Check your answers in the Appendix.

1. _____ (seven words)

   Listen for the contraction *I'd*.

2. _____ (six words)

   Listen for the contraction *I'll*.

3. _____ (eight words)

   Listen for the reduced vowel sound in *going to*.

4. _____ (four words)

   Listen for the contraction *haven't*.

5. _____ (six words)

   Listen for the reduced vowel sound in *and*.

Exercise 3

Listen as your teacher reads you the clues to the word puzzle. Write the words in the blanks after each number. Check your answers in the Appendix.

1.   C __ __ __ __ __

2.   H __ __ __ __ __

3.   I __ __

4.   C __ __ __ __

5. __ __ __ __ K

6.   __ __ E

7.   __ __ __ N

10   Talking About Money

Notes

1. Put It In the Bank

This chant provides practice in the reduced vowel sound of *it* and offers examples of two-word verbs, *put in* and *take out.* It provides practice in the command forms *save/spend/take/put.*

1   Put It In the Bank ★

Save it.
Save it.
Put it in the bank.
Save it.
Save it.
Put it in the bank.
      Spend it.
      Take it out of the bank.
      Spend it.
      Take it out of the bank.
Save it.
      Spend it.
Save it.
      Spend it.
Save it.
      Spend it.
Put it in the bank.

2. How Much Does It Cost? It Costs a Lot

This chant provides examples of the reduced vowel sounds in *does, it,* and *to* and the sound and use of the indefinite articles *a/an* as illustrated in *a lot/an awful.* It also offers practice in the third person *s* in *costs* and the plural *s* in *days.*

2   How Much Does It Cost? It Costs a Lot ★

How much does it cost?
      It costs a lot.
How much does it cost?
      It costs a lot.
      I can't believe how much it costs.
It costs a lot, an awful lot.

It costs a lot to live in the city.
      How much does it cost?
It costs a lot.
It costs a lot to eat out these days.
      How much does it cost?
It costs a lot.

3 Why Don't You Buy It? I Can't Afford It ⋆

Why don't you buy it?
      I can't afford it.
      It's too expensive.
      I can't afford it.

Why don't you buy it?
      I don't have the money.
      It's not worth it.
      I can't afford it.

4 Pennies, Nickels, Dimes, and Quarters ⋆

Pennies, nickels, dimes, and quarters.
Pennies, nickels, dimes, and quarters.
How many pennies in a nickel?
      Five.
How many nickels in a dime?
      Two.

Pennies, nickels, dimes, and quarters.
Pennies, nickels, dimes, and quarters.
How many dimes in a dollar?
      Ten.
How many nickels in a dime?
      Two.

Pennies, nickels, dimes, and quarters.
Pennies, nickels, dimes, and quarters.
How many quarters in a dollar?
      Four.
How many nickels in a dime?
      Two.

5 I'll Get It. Oh No, I'll Get It ★

(two friends arguing over the check)

I'll get it.
　　　　Oh no, *I'll* get it.
Let *me* have it.
It's *my* turn.
　　　　I'll get it.
Oh no, *I'll* get it.
　　　　Let *me* have it.
　　　　It's *my* turn.

You got it last time.
I'll get it this time.
　　　　Let *me* have it.
　　　　It's *my* turn.
You got it last time.
I'll get it this time.
　　　　Let *me* have it.
　　　　It's *my* turn.

Let's split it.
Let's split it.
Let's split it this time.
Let's split it.
　　　　You got it last time.
　　　　I'll get it next time.
　　　　This time,
　　　　let's split it.

Unit 10 Exercises

Exercise 1

Listen carefully as your teacher reads the sentences. Then listen again as your teacher repeats them. Fill in the blanks with the correct words. Check your answers in the Appendix.

1. It _____ _____ lot _____ live _____

   _____ city.

2. _____ much _____ _____ cost?

3. _____ costs _____ _____ lot.

4. Why _____ you _____ _____ ?

5. _____ too _____ . I _____ afford

   _____ .

Exercise 2

Listen carefully while your teacher reads the sentences. Write them in the blanks below. Note the suggestions for careful listening. Check your answers in the Appendix.

1. _____ (nine words)

   Listen for the third person *s* and the plural *s*.

2. _____ (four words)

   Listen for the contraction and the reduced vowel sound.

3. _____ (seven words)

   Listen for the sound of the contraction and the third person *s*.

4. _____ (five words)

   Listen for the sound of the contraction and the reduced vowel sound.

5. _____ (five words)

   Listen for the reduced vowel sound.

Exercise 3

Listen as your teacher reads you the clues to the word puzzle. Write the words in the blanks after each number. Check your answers in the Appendix.

1. **M** ___ ___ ___ ___

2. **O** ___ ___

3. **N** ___ ___ ___ ___

4. **E** ___ ___ ___

5. **Y** ___ ___ ___

11   Talking About the Weather

Notes

1. It's Cold Outside. It's Bitter Cold
This chant offers practice in the command forms *bundle up, put on,* and *wear something* and in the sound of the contraction *it's.*

1   It's Cold Outside. It's Bitter Cold

It's cold outside.
It's bitter cold.
      Put on your sweater.
      It's bitter cold.
It's cold outside.
It's bitter cold.
      Wear something warm.
      It's bitter cold.
It's cold outside.
It's bitter cold.
      It's freezing.
      Wear something warm.
Bundle up.
It's cold outside.
      Wear something warm.
      It's bitter cold.

2. It's a Nice Day Today, Isn't It?
This chant offers practice in the tag ending *isn't it* followed by the response *It certainly is.* Students should listen for the reduced vowel sound in *today* and the linking sounds of *day today/isn't it.*

2   It's a Nice Day Today, Isn't It? ★

It's a nice day today, isn't it?
      It certainly is.
      It's a beautiful day.
It's a nice day today, isn't it?
      It certainly is.
      It's a beautiful day.

Nice day today.
Nice day today.
Day today.
Day today.
Nice day today.

Nice day today, isn't it?
      It certainly is.
      It's a beautiful day.

3 Hot and Humid

It's hot today.
          Hot and humid.
It's hot today, isn't it?

It's hot today.
          Hot and humid.
It's hot today, isn't it?
          It sure is.
          It sure is.
          Hot and humid.
          Hot and humid.

Too hot.
Much too hot.
          Too hot.
          Much too hot.
It's too hot to work.
Too hot to play.
Too hot to walk to work today.
It's too hot.
          Hot and humid.
Too hot.
          Hot and humid.
Too hot to work.
Too hot to play.
Too hot to walk to work today.

4 Clear, Blue Sky

Clear, blue sky.
Clear, blue sky.
Look at the sky.
It's clear as a bell.
Clear, blue sky.

It's beautiful today.
Not a cloud in the sky.
Clear, blue sky.

Look at the sky.
It's clear as a bell.
Clear, blue sky.

5. **Do You Think It's Going to Rain?**
This chant offers an example of the reduction in the sound of *going to* (gonna). It also provides practice in the sound of the third person *s* and illustrates the use of *I hope so/I hope not.*

5 Do You Think It's Going to Rain? ★

Do you think it's going to rain?
　　　　I hope not.
Do you think it's going to rain?
　　　　I hope not.
It looks like rain.
It looks like rain.
Do you think it's going to rain?
　　　　I hope not.

Do you think it's going to snow?
　　　　I hope so.
Do you think it's going to snow?
　　　　I hope so.
It looks like snow.
It looks like snow.
Do you think it's going to snow?
　　　　I hope so.

Unit 11 Exercises

Exercise 1

Listen carefully as your teacher reads the sentences. Then listen again as your teacher repeats them. Fill in the blanks with the correct words. Check your answers in the Appendix.

1. _____ _____ nice _____ today,
_____ it?

2. It _____ is. It's _____ beautiful
_____ .

3. It's _____ hot _____ walk _____ work
_____ .

4. _____ much _____ hot, _____ and
_____ .

5. Look _____ the _____ . _____ clear
_____ _____ bell.

6. Do _____ think _____ going _____ rain?

7. Put _____ your _____ . _____
bitter _____ .

8. _____ something _____ . _____ cold
_____ .

9. _____ freezing. Do _____ think _____ going
_____ snow?

10. I _____ not.

58

Exercise 2

Listen carefully while your teacher reads the sentences. Write them in the blanks below. Note the suggestions for careful listening. Check your answers in the Appendix.

1. _____

_____ (six words; two sentences)

   Listen for the contractions.

2. _____

_____ (five words; two sentences)

   Listen for the contraction and the -ing sounds.

3. _____ (seven words)

   Listen for the reduced vowel sound in going to and the contraction.

4. _____ (seven words)

   Listen for the contraction and the reduced vowel sound in to.

5. _____ (seven words)

   Listen for the contractions and the reduced vowel sounds in a/today/it.

Exercise 3

Listen as your teacher reads you the clues to the word puzzle. Write the words in the blanks after each number. Check your answers in the Appendix.

1.   W ___ ___ ___

2. ___ ___ ___ ___ ___   E

3.   A ___ ___ ___ ___ ___

4.   T ___ ___

5.   H ___ ___

6.   E ___ ___

7.   R ___ ___ ___

12 Asking For and Giving Information

Notes

1. How Long Does It Take?
This chant provides an example of the high frequency information question, *How long does it take?* It also offers practice in the third person *s*, as in *takes*, and the plural *s* in the vocabulary items *hours*, *days*, and *months*. Students should notice the sound of the contraction *that's* and the vowel reduction in *does*.

2. Downtown Bus
This chant offers examples of yes/no questions using *is this/does this* and the accompanying short responses, *Yes, it is/Yes, it does.*

1 How Long Does It Take? ★

How long does it take?
      It takes a long time.
How long does it take?
      It takes a long time.
How long does it take?
      It takes a long time.
      It takes a long, long time.

It takes twenty-four hours.
      That's a long time.
It takes fifteen days.
      That's a long time.
It takes three and a half months.
      That's a long time.
      That's a long, long time.

2 Downtown Bus

Downtown.
Downtown bus.
Downtown.
Downtown bus.
      Is this the downtown bus?
Yes, it is.
      Is this the downtown bus?
Yes, it is.
      Is this the downtown bus?
Yes, it is.
      Does this bus go downtown?
Yes.
Yes, it does.
Downtown.
Downtown bus.
Downtown.
Downtown bus.
      Is this the downtown bus?
Yes, it is.
      Does this bus go downtown?
Yes!

3. Walk Two Blocks and Turn Right
This chant provides an example of yes/no questions with *is there . . . .* Students should note the use of the indefinite article *a,* the plural *s* in *blocks* and the sound of the contraction *can't.* This chant also offers practice in the sound of the vowel reduction in *it* and the vocabulary items for giving simple directions, *turn left/turn right/walk two blocks.*

3 **Walk Two Blocks and Turn Right**

Is there a bank near here?
> Yes, there is.
> Walk two blocks and turn right.

Is there a phone near here?
> Yes, there is.
> Walk two blocks and turn right.

Is there a newspaper stand near here?
> Yes, there is.
> Yes, there is.
> Walk two blocks and turn right.

Is there a coffee shop near here?
> Yes, there is.
> Yes, there is.
> Walk two blocks and turn left.

> Turn left. Turn left.
> Walk two blocks and turn left.
> Turn right. Turn right.
> Walk two blocks and turn right.
> You can't miss it.

4. Who? What? When? Where? Why?

This chant offers practice in the sound of the high frequency question words. Students should notice the sound of the reduced vowel in *did* as it occurs in the question *What did he do?* contrasted with the full sound of *did* when it is given stress in *Who did it*?

4 Who? What? When? Where? Why? ★

Who?
What?
When?
Where?
Why? Why?

Who?
What?
When?
Where?
Why? Why?

Who did it?
What did he do?
      Where did he do it?
      Why?
Who did it?
What did he do?
      Where did he do it?
      Why?
Who did it?
What did he do?
      Who did it?
      What did he do?
Who did it?
What did he do?
      Where did he do it?
      Why?

5. **Is the Post Office Open Tomorrow?**

This chant provides examples of yes/no and information questions, *Is the post office open . . . / What time does it open?* Students should practice the sound of the contractions *it's* and *they're* and should note the third person *s* in *opens/closes*, the plural *s* in *stores*, and the vowel reductions in the sounds of *from, to, tomorrow, does,* and *at.* This chant also illustrates the use of the definite article *the* in *the post office/the stores.*

5 Is the Post Office Open Tomorrow?

Is the post office open tomorrow?
　　　It's open from nine to five.
Is the post office open tomorrow?
　　　It's open from nine to five.
What time does it open?
　　　It opens at nine.
What time does it close?
　　　It closes at five.
　　　It opens at nine and closes at five.
　　　It's open from nine to five.

Are the stores open tomorrow?
　　　They're open from nine to five.
Are the stores open tomorrow?
　　　They're open from nine to five.
When do they open?
　　　They open at nine.
When do they close?
　　　They close at five.
Are the stores open tomorrow?
　　　They're open from nine to five.

Unit 12 Exercises

Exercise 1

Listen carefully as your teacher reads the sentences. Then listen again as your teacher repeats them. Fill in the blanks with the correct words. Check your answers in the Appendix.

1. _____ long _____ _____ take?

2. It _____ _____ long _____ .

3. Does _____ bus _____ downtown?

4. Is _____ a _____ stand _____ here?

5. Yes, _____ _____ . _____ two _____

   and _____ left.

6. _____ the _____ _____ open

   _____ ?

7. _____ open _____ nine _____ five.

8. When _____ it _____ ?

9. It _____ at _____ .

10. _____ the _____ open _____ ?

Exercise 2

Listen carefully while your teacher reads the sentences. Write them in the blanks below. Note the suggestions for careful listening. Check your answers in the Appendix.

1. _____ (five words)
   Listen for the plural *s* and the reduced vowel sounds.

2. _____ (seven words)
   Listen for the sound of the indefinite article *a*.

3. _____

   _____ (nine words; two sentences)
   Listen for the plural *s* and the reduced vowel sound in *and*.

4. _____ (five words)
   Listen for the reduced vowel sounds in *does/it*.

5. _____ (seven words)
   Listen for the third person *s*, the plural *s*, and the reduced vowel sounds.

Exercise 3

Listen as your teacher reads you the clues to the word puzzle. Write the words in the blanks after each number. Check your answers in the Appendix.

1.   W ___ ___
2.   H ___ ___
3.   ___ ___ E ___
4.   ___ ___ ___ R ___
5. ___ ___ ___ ___ E

Exercise 4

Listen carefully as your teacher reads you the facts. Then answer the questions below. Check your answers in the Appendix.

1. If you leave New York on a midnight flight to San Francisco, what time will you arrive (California time)?

2. My brother called me from San Francisco. He said his flight to New York was leaving in 15 minutes. I met him at the airport in New York at 4:00 in the afternoon. What time did he make the phone call (California time)?

1. _____

2. _____

13 Giving and Receiving Thanks

Notes

1. Thank You Very Much
This chant presents some examples of the ritual language of thanking and receiving thanks. Students should also note the sound of the contraction *you're* and the reduced vowel in *it* as it occurs in *I appreciate it.*

1 Thank You Very Much

Thank you very much.
  You're welcome.
Thank you very much.
I appreciate it.
Thank you very much.
  You're welcome.
Thank you very much.
I appreciate it.

Thank you.
Thank you very much.
Thank you.
Thank you very much.
Thank you.
Thank you very much.
I appreciate it.
  You're welcome.

2. Thanks a Lot
This chant provides examples of the plural *s* in *thanks* and the sound of the indefinite article *a*. Students should note the vowel reductions in *for*, *it*, *was*, and *to* and the sound of the contractions *don't* and *you're*.

2 Thanks a Lot

Thanks a lot.
Thanks a lot.
Thanks a lot for everything.
  Don't mention it.
  I was happy to do it.

Thanks a million.
Thanks a lot.
Thanks a lot for everything.
  You're welcome.
  I was happy to do it.

Thanks a million.
Thanks a lot.
Thanks a million.
Thanks a lot.
Thanks a million.
Thanks a lot.
  You're welcome.
  I was happy to do it.

3. Thank You So Much. It's Just What I Wanted
This chant offers practice in the sound of the contractions *it's* and *I'm* and the use of *just* and **so** for emphasis.

3 Thank You So Much. It's Just What I Wanted

(thanking someone for a gift)

Thank you so much.
It's just what I wanted.
       I'm glad you like it.
       I'm *so* glad you like it.
It's just what I wanted.
       I'm glad you like it.
It's just the right size.
       I'm glad you like it.
It's just the right color.
       I'm glad you like it.
It's just what I wanted.
       I'm glad you like it.
It's perfect.
       I'm *so* glad.
I love it.
       I'm glad.

4. That Was Awfully Nice Of You
This chant illustrates the use of **awfully/very/so** for emphasis and provides examples of the contraction *I'm* and the reduced vowel sounds in *was, to,* and *it*.

4 That Was Awfully Nice Of You

(thanking someone for doing a favor)

That was *awfully* nice of you.
       I'm glad I was able to help.
That was *very* nice of you.
       I'm glad I was able to help.
That was *so* nice.
       I'm glad I could do it.
That was *very* nice.
       I'm glad I could do it.
That was *awfully* nice.
       I'm glad I could do it.
       I'm glad I was able to help.

       I'm glad I could do it.
       I'm *so* glad.
       I'm glad I could do it.
       I'm *so* glad.
       I'm glad I could do it.
       I'm *so* glad.
       I'm glad I was able to help.

5   Thanks Again

Thanks again.
        Any time.
Thanks again.
        It was my pleasure.
Thanks again.
        Don't mention it.
Thanks again.
        You're welcome.
Thanks again.
        I enjoyed doing it.
Thanks again.
        Thank *you*.

Thanks again.
You shouldn't have done it.
        I wanted to.
        The pleasure was mine.

Unit 13 Exercises

Exercise 1

Listen carefully as your teacher reads the sentences. Then listen again as your teacher repeats them. Fill in the blanks with the correct words. Check your answers in the Appendix.

1. _____ you _____ much. _____ just

   _____ I _____ .

2. I'm _____ you _____ it.

3. _____ was _____ nice _____ you.

4. _____ glad I _____ able _____ help.

5. Thanks _____ . I _____ it.

6. Don't _____ it. It _____ my _____ .

7. You _____ have _____ it.

8. I _____ to. The _____ was _____ .

Exercise 2

Listen carefully while your teacher reads the sentences. Write them in the blanks below. Note the suggestions for careful listening. Check your answers in the Appendix.

1. _____ (five words)

   Listen for the plural s.

2. _____ (five words)

   Listen for the contraction and the reduced vowel sounds in *have/it*.

3. _____ (six words)

   Listen for the reduced vowel sounds.

4. _____ (six words)

   Listen for the sound of the contraction and the reduced vowel sound in *it*.

5. _____ (five words)

   Listen for the sound of the contraction and the reduced vowel sounds.

Exercise 3

Guest of Honor

One person in the class is chosen as the "guest of honor." The other students look at the list of gifts below and choose one they would like to give the "guest of honor." Each student writes the name of the gift on a piece of paper, folds it, signs it, and gives it to the "guest of honor," who will then open all the gifts and thank each person in an appropriate manner. Look at the example.

Example

(a diamond ring)

Guest of honor: Thanks a million. I love it!
Giver: I'm glad you like it.

Gifts

a cheap umbrella
a pair of pink pajamas
a beautiful black car
a tired old dog
a box of chocolates
a diamond ring
a red lace dress
a white sailboat
a one-way ticket to Paris for two
a vacuum cleaner

Exercise 4

Listen as your teacher reads you the clues to the word puzzle. Write the words in the blanks after each number. Check your answers in the Appendix.

1. T ___ ___ ___ ___

2. H ___ ___ ___ ___

3. A ___ ___ ___ ___

4. N ___ ___ ___

5. K ___ ___ ___

6. S ___ ___ ___ ___ ___ ___ ___

14 Expressing Confusion

Notes

1. This Is Confusing. I'm Very Confused

This chant offers practice in the pronunciation of the contractions *I'm, can't, he's,* and *it's.* It provides examples of the contrasting forms *confusing/confused.* Students should note that a person is *confused* and a situation or object is *confusing.* This chant also provides an example of the contrast in the sound of *can/can't* and the disappearing *h* in *he's (what he's saying)* and in *him (understand him).*

2. Who Has the Keys?

This chant provides practice in the plural forms *keys/tickets/them* and in a shifting stress pattern *I thought* **you** *had them/I gave them to* **you.** Students should note the past tense form of irregular verbs, *thought* and *gave,* and the use of the definite article, *the keys/the tickets/the money.*

1 This Is Confusing. I'm Very Confused

This is confusing.
I'm very confused.
I can't understand what he's saying, can *you*?

This is confusing.
I'm very confused.
I can't understand what he's saying.

I'm all mixed up.
I'm all mixed up.

It's very confusing.
I can't understand him.
He's talking too quickly.
I can't understand him.

This is confusing.
I'm very confused.
I can't understand what he's saying.

2 Who Has the Keys? ★

Who has the keys?
            What keys?
My keys.
            I thought *you* had them.
I gave them to *you*.

            Who has the tickets?
What tickets?
            Our tickets.
I thought *you* had them.
            I gave them to *you*.

Who has the money?
            What money?
My money.
            I thought *you* had it.
I gave it to *you*.

71

3. Does This Make Sense to You?
This chant provides practice in shifting stress for emphasis, *Does this make sense to you?* It offers examples of the *can/can't* sounds and provides practice in the short tag endings *do you/can you.* It also offers practice in the use of *neither/so* as it occurs in *Neither can I, Neither do I,* and *So am I.* Students should note the use of *totally* in place of *very.*

4. Where Do We Go?
This chant provides practice in the question forms with *what do/shall* and *where do/is/shall.* It also offers examples of the contractions *don't, where's,* and *I'm.* This chant includes useful expressions, *I'm not quite sure/I was counting on **you**.*

3 Does This Make Sense to You? ★

Does this make sense to you?
        No. Does it make any sense to you?
No. I can't figure it out, can you?
        No, I can't.
Neither can I.
I don't understand this at all, do you?
        No, I don't.
Neither do I.
I'm very confused.
        I am too.
I'm totally lost.
        So am I.

4 Where Do We Go? ★

Where do we go?
What do we do?
        Don't ask *me*.
        I was following *you*.

What do we do?
Where do we go?
        Don't ask *me*.
        I don't know.

Where's the hotel?
Where's the car?
        I'm not quite sure
        just where we are.

Where shall we go?
What shall we do?
        Don't ask *me*.
        I was counting on *you*.

5. **What Are We Supposed to Do?**
This chant provides practice in the
use of *supposed to* with the
question words *what/when/where*. It
also offers practice in the sound of
the past tense in *thought* and *knew*
and the reduced vowels in *are*, *to*,
and *am*.

5   What Are We Supposed to Do?

What are we supposed to do?
      I thought you knew.
What are we supposed to do?
      I thought you knew.
When are we supposed to go?
Where are we supposed to be?
What are we supposed to do?
      I thought you knew.

What am I supposed to do?
      I thought you knew.
What am I supposed to do?
      I thought you knew.

When am I supposed to go?
Where am I supposed to be?
What am I supposed to do?
      I thought you knew.

Unit 14 Exercises

Exercise 1

Listen carefully as your teacher reads the sentences. Then listen again as your teacher repeats them. Fill in the blanks with the correct words. Check your answers in the Appendix.

1. _____ is _____ . I _____ understand

   _____ he's _____ , can _____ ?

2. No, I _____ . He's _____ too _____ .

3. _____ very _____ . I _____

   understand _____ .

4. I'm _____ lost.

5. _____ am _____ . I'm _____ mixed _____ .

6. _____ the _____ ? _____ do _____ go?

7. _____ not _____ sure _____ where

   _____ are.

8. What _____ we _____ ?

9. _____ ask _____ . I _____ counting

   _____ you.

10. I _____ you _____ .

74

Exercise 2

Listen carefully while your teacher reads the sentences. Write them in the blanks below. Note the suggestions for careful listening. Check your answers in the Appendix.

1. _____

   _____ (seven words; two sentences)

   Listen for the sound of the contraction and the disappearing *h* in *him*.

2. _____ (six words)

   Listen for the plural *s*.

3. _____ (seven words)

   Listen for the contrasting sounds in *can/can't*.

4. _____ (eight words)

   Listen for the sound of the contraction.

5. _____ (six words)

   Listen for the reduced vowel sounds in *are/to*.

Exercise 3

Listen carefully while your teacher reads the problems. Take notes and figure out the answers. The complete problems and the Answer Key appear in the Appendix.

1. $ _____

2. _____ years old

3. _____

4. _____ years old

5. _____ years old

15   Making Plans

Notes

1. What Are You Going to Do?
This chant offers practice in the future with *going to* and the shifting stress pattern in *What are you going to do/What are **you** going to do?* It also includes examples of plural *s* in *plans* and the third person *s* in *depends*. Students should note the vowel reduction in the sound of *going to* (gonna).

1   What Are You Going to Do?

What are you going to do when you finish this course?
         I'm not quite sure.
         What are *you* going to do?
I'm not quite sure.
I haven't decided.

What are your plans?
Are you going to stay here?
         I'm not quite sure.
         Are *you* going to stay?
It all depends.
I'm not quite sure.
         Are you going to get a job?
It all depends.
         Are you going to buy a car?
It all depends.
         Are you going to take a trip?
It all depends.
I'm not quite sure.
I'm not quite sure.

2. Let's Make a Date
This chant offers practice in the sound of the contractions *let's, I'm, that's, I'll, I'd,* and *eight's.* Students should note the vowel reductions in the sound of *tomorrow, at, to, together,* and *for.*

2   Let's Make a Date

Let's make a date.
Are you busy tomorrow?
         I'm free at two.
         What about you?
That's fine with me.
I'll meet you at two.

I'd love to see you.
When are you free?
         Call me tomorrow.
         I finish at three.

Can we get together tomorrow at three?
         I'm sorry, that's a little too early for me.
         How about eight?
That's a little too late.
I'm sorry, but eight's just a little too late.

3. How About Nine?
This chant offers practice in the
sound of the contractions *that's, it's,*
and *eight's.* It provides examples of
the language of suggestion, *what
about . . ./how about . . . .* and useful
expressions such as *That's fine with
me/It's up to you/The later the
better/Whatever you say.*

3   How About Nine?

How about nine?
      Nine is fine.
How about three?
      That's fine with me.

How about two?
      It's up to you.

How about eight?
      Eight's too late.

Is eight too late?
      Not at all.
      The later the better.
What about nine?
      Nine is fine.

Is two OK?
      Whatever you say.
Is three OK?
What about three?
      Whatever you say
      is fine with me.

4. I've Got So Much to Do Today
This chant provides examples of the
use of *much* and *many.* It also
offers practice in the sound of the
reduced vowel in *to* and *today,* the
plural *s* in *things* and the
contractions *I've* and *don't.*

4   I've Got So Much to Do Today

I've got so much to do today,
So much to do.
So much to do today.
So much to do.
I've got so much to do.
I don't know what to do first.

I've got so much to do.
I don't know what to do first.
I've got so much to do.
I don't know where to begin.
I've got so much to do.
I don't know where to begin.

I've got so many things to do.
I've got so many things to do.
I've got so much to do.
So many things to do.
So many things to do.
So much to do.

5 Will You Be Here Next Year? ★

Will you be here next year?
   I will, if all goes well.
   If all goes well, I will.
   Yes, I will, if all goes well.
What'll you do if it doesn't go well?
   If it doesn't go well,
   I won't be here.
   What about you?
   What are you going to do?
I haven't decided.
What about you?

Unit 15 Exercises

Exercise 1

Listen carefully as your teacher reads the sentences. Then listen again as your teacher repeats them. Fill in the blanks with the correct words. Check your answers in the Appendix.

1. What _____ _____ _____ _____

   do _____ you finish _____ course?

2. _____ not _____ sure. What _____ _____

   going _____ do?

3. I _____ decided. What _____ you?

4. _____ all _____ .

5. _____ we get _____ tomorrow _____

   three?

6. I'm _____ , that's _____ little _____

   early _____ me. How _____ eight?

7. _____ a _____ too _____ .

8. _____ love _____ see _____ . _____ are

   you _____ ?

9. _____ me _____ . I _____ at

   _____ . _____ three _____ ?

10. _____ you _____ is _____ with

    _____ .

Exercise 2

Listen carefully while your teacher reads the sentences. Write them in the blanks below. Note the suggestions for careful listening. Check your answers in the Appendix.

1. _____ (four words)

   Listen for the sound of the contraction and the indefinite article *a*.

2. _____. (five words)

   Listen for the sound of the contraction and the reduced vowel sounds.

3. _____ (seven words)

   Listen for the reduced vowel sounds.

4. _____

   _____ (thirteen words)

   Listen for the sound of the contractions and the reduced vowel sound in *to*.

5. _____ (eight words)

   Listen for the sound of the contractions.

Exercise 3

Which Should I Do First?

Listen carefully while your teacher reads a list of three activities and put them in the *logically* correct order. The complete lists of activities appear in the Appendix.

A 1. _____

   2. _____

   3. _____

B 1. _____

   2. _____

   3. _____

C 1. _____

   2. _____

   3. _____

D 1._____

   2. _____

   3. _____

Appendix

UNIT 1

Exercise 1

1. *Hi*, Mary. *How's your* mother?
2. *She's* fine, thank you. *How's* Bill?
3. *He's* fine. *How are the* children?
4. *They're* fine. *How's your* job?
5. *It's* fine. *It's so* good *to* see *you*.
6. *It's* good *to see* you.
7. *I'm so* glad *you're* back.
8. *So am* I. I *haven't seen* you *for a* long *time*.

Exercise 2

1. How's your job?
2. It's so good to see you.
3. How've you been?
4. I haven't seen you for a long time.
5. I'm so glad you're back.

UNIT 2

Exercise 1

1. Harry, *I'd* like *you to* meet *my* sister Mary.
2. How *do you do*, Mary. *I'm* very *glad to* meet *you*.
3. *Thank* you. *I'm* glad *to meet* you. *I've* heard *so* much *about* you.
4. How *long have* you *been* here?
5. *I've* been *here* for *a* long *time*.
6. Bill, *I'd* like *you to* meet *my* friend Jane.
7. *Hi*, Jane. *I've* heard *so* many *nice things* about *you*.
8. Thank you. Where *are you from*?
9. *I'm from* New York.
10. *So am* I.

Exercise 3

1. I've heard so many nice things about you.
2. How long have you been here?
3. I'm very glad to meet you.
4. How do you pronounce your first name?
5. How do you spell it?

UNIT 3

Exercise 1

1. *Bye-bye. See* you *tomorrow*.
2. *So* long. Have *a* nice *weekend*.
3. *It's getting* late and *I've* got *to go* home.
4. I *really* hate *to say* good-bye.
5. It *was* nice *seeing* you *again*.
6. *Say* hello *to* Jack. Tell *him* I miss *him*.
7. Say *hello to* Mary. *Tell her* I *miss her*.
8. *We're* going *to* miss you. We *really* are.
9. *I'm going to* miss *you too*. I *really* am.
10. Please *don't* go. I'm *really* going *to miss* you.

Exercise 2

1. I've got to go home.
2. Tell him I miss him.
3. Good-bye, Harry, say hello to Mary.
4. I'm going to miss you.
5. It was nice seeing you.

Exercise 3

1. I'm thinking of a word that starts with G.
   It has four letters.
   It's very expensive.
   It's very beautiful.
   Wedding rings are made of this.
   (Answer: *gold*)

2. I'm thinking of a word that has three letters.
   It's something that everybody will someday be,
      and lots of people already are.
   It starts with O.
   It's the opposite of **young**.
   (Answer: *old*)

3. I'm thinking of a word that ends with O.
   It has three letters.
   It's bigger than **one**.
   It's a number.
   It rhymes with **blue**.
   (Answer: *two*)

4. I'm thinking of a word that ends with D.
   It has four letters.
   It has two legs.
   It flies.
   Sometimes it sings.
   (Answer: *bird*)

5. I'm thinking of a word that starts with B.
   It has four letters.
   It's a part of your body.
   Sometimes it hurts.
   Many people lie on it when they sleep.
   (Answer: *back*)

6. I'm thinking of a word that starts with Y.
   It has six letters.
   It's a color.
   Sometimes cats' eyes are this color.
   It's the color of some flowers.
   It's the color of a lemon.
   (Answer: *yellow*)

7. I'm thinking of a word that starts with E.
   It's a little word.
   It has three letters.
   It ends in D.
   It means **no more**.
   (Answer: *end*)

1.   **G** **O** **L** **D**
2.   **O** **L** **D**
3. **T** **W** **O**
4. **B** **I** **R** **D**
5.   **B** **A** **C** **K**
6.   **Y** **E** **L** **L** **O** **W**
7.   **E** **N** **D**

UNIT 4

Exercise 1

1. You *look* wonderful *today*.
2. Thanks, *so do* you.
3. *That's a* nice *color* on *you*.
4. *I'm* glad *you* like *it*.
5. *That's a* nice *sweater*. Is *it* new?
6. Oh no. *I've* had *it for* years.
7. *It's* beautiful.
8. You *haven't* changed *a bit*.
9. I *like your* gloves. Are *they* new?
10. Yes, *they* are. I *got them at* Macy's.

Exercise 2

1. That's a nice sweater.
2. Where did you get it?
3. I got it at Macy's.
4. That's a nice color on you.
5. Those are nice boots.
6. Where did you get them?
7. I got them at Macy's.
8. They're beautiful.
9. Thanks a lot.
10. I'm glad you like them.

Exercise 3

1. I'm thinking of a word that starts with G.
   It has five letters.
   It's the color of spring.
   It's the color of grass, trees, and leaves.
   (Answer: *green*)

2. I'm thinking of a word that starts with R.
   It has three letters.
   It means **stop**.
   It's the color of fire.
   (Answer: *red*)

3. I'm thinking of a word that ends in E.
   It has five letters.
   It's the color of a cloud, an egg, and sometimes a rabbit.
   It's the opposite of **black**.
   (Answer: *white*)

4. I'm thinking of a word that ends in E.
   It has four letters.
   It's the color of the sky.
   It's the color of a ribbon for a baby boy.
   (Answer: *blue*)

5. I'm thinking of a word that ends in N.
   It has five letters.
   Sometimes beautiful eyes are this color.
   It's the color of wood.
   (Answer: *brown*)

1.   **G** **R** **E** **E** **N**
2.   **R** **E** **D**
3. **W** **H** **I** **T** **E**
4.   **B** **L** **U** **E**
5. **B** **R** **O** **W** **N**

UNIT 5

Exercise 1

1. *Let's have* lunch *today*.
2. *Can you* come *over for a* drink *tonight*?
3. *I'd* love *to*. *What* time *should* I *come*?
4. *We're* having *a* party *next* Saturday *night*. I *hope you* can *come*.
5. I *wish* I *could* but I'm *afraid* I *can't*.
6. *When's the* best *time to* call *you*?
7. I'm *usually* home *after* seven.
8. You *call* me *or I'll* call *you*.
9. I *feel* like *going to the* movies *tonight*.
10. I *do too*. *Let's* go.

Exercise 4

1. I'm thinking of a word that starts with P.
   It has six letters.
   It's a word that you say when you want to be polite.
   (Answer: *please*)

2. I'm thinking of a word that starts with A.
   It has five letters.
   It means there is no one else with you.
   (Answer: *alone*)

3. I'm thinking of a word that starts with R.
   It has five letters.
   The last letter is T.
   It's the opposite of **left**.
   It's the opposite of **wrong**.
   (Answer: *right*)

4. I'm thinking of a word that starts with T.
   It has five letters.
   It's how you feel at the end of a long, long day.
   (Answer: *tired*)

5. I'm thinking of a word that starts with Y.
   It has nine letters.
   It's what today will be tomorrow.
   (Answer: *yesterday*)

1. **P** **L** **E** **A** **S** **E**
2. **A** **L** **O** **N** **E**
3. **R** **I** **G** **H** **T**
4. **T** **I** **R** **E** **D**
5. **Y** **E** **S** **T** **E** **R** **D** **A** **Y**

UNIT 6

Exercise 1

1. I *like it a* lot.
2. *I'm* glad *you* like *it*.
3. *I'm* afraid *it's* not *quite* right.
4. I *really* like *it* very *much*.
5. *It's* all *right*, I *guess*.

6. Will *this* be *OK*?
7. *It'll* have *to do*.
8. Are *you* sure *it's* OK?
9. I *can't* stand *it*.
10. *I'm* sorry *you* feel *that* way.

Exercise 2

1. I really like it very much.
2. I'm afraid it's not quite right.
3. I don't like it a bit.
4. I can't stand it.
5. I guess it's all right.

UNIT 7

Exercise 1

1. I *give up*. I *can't* do *it*.
2. I *read it* once. I *couldn't* understand *it*.
3. *Will* I *ever* learn *to* speak English?
4. *Of* course *you* will. *You're* getting *better* all *the* time.
5. *Don't* give *up*. Try *it* again.
6. *Am* I *doing* all *right*?
7. *Of* course *you are*. *You're* doing *fine*.
8. Can *she* speak French?
9. *Of* course *she* can. *It's her* native *language*.
10. She *was* born *in* France.

Exercise 2

1. I give up. I can't do it.
2. Don't give up. Try it again.
3. You can do it just as well as I can.
4. Believe me, it's not that hard.
5. You're getting better all the time.

Exercise 3

1. Bob can go with us.
2. We can't leave on Thursday.
3. We can leave on Thursday.
4. I can't help you with that problem.
5. They can do it easily.
6. She can't come to your dinner party.
7. He can give you a lesson tomorrow.
8. I can't be there before ten.
9. I can be there before ten.
10. Bob can't go with us.

UNIT 8

Exercise 1

1. I'm *terribly* sorry. It *was* my *mistake*.
2. *That's* all *right*. Don't *worry* about *it*.
3. *It's* all *my* fault. I *shouldn't have* done *it*.
4. *Don't* be *silly*. You *couldn't* help *it*.
5. I *should* have *told* you.
6. It *doesn't* matter. *Honestly*, it *doesn't*.
7. I'm *afraid* I *owe* you *an* apology.
8. I'm *sorry* about *last* night.
9. Don't *be* silly. *There's* nothing to *apologize* for.
10. Please *excuse* me. I *shouldn't* have *taken* it.

Exercise 2

1. That's all right. It doesn't matter.
2. Don't worry about it.

3. I shouldn't have done it.
4. I should have told you.
5. I owe you an apology.

UNIT 9

Exercise 1

1. I think *I'll* have *a* large *bowl of* chicken soup *today*.
2. What *are* you *going to* have?
3. I think *I'll* have *the* same.
4. What *are* you *going to* drink?
5. I *haven't* decided *yet*.
6. *I'd* like *a* tuna salad *sandwich on* whole *wheat* toast.
7. That *sounds* good.
8. Pass *the* bread *and* butter, *please*.
9. Please *pass the* pepper, *please* pass *the* salt.
10. *I'd* like rice *and beans*.

Exercise 2

1. I'd like a large cup of soup.
2. I think I'll have the same.
3. What are you going to have for dessert?
4. I haven't decided yet.
5. Pass the bread and butter, please.

Exercise 3

1. I'm thinking of a word that starts with C.
It has six letters.
It's wonderful in a sandwich.
You can use it to catch mice.
(Answer: *cheese*)

2. I'm thinking of a word that starts with H.
It has six letters.
It's the way you feel when you don't eat.
Many people feel this way when they wake up.
(Answer: *hungry*)

3. I'm thinking of a word that starts with I.
It has three letters.
It rhymes with **nice**.
It's very cold.
(Answer: *ice*)

4. I'm thinking of a word that starts with C.
It has five letters.
It's rich but fattening.
Some people put it in their coffee.
(Answer: *cream*)

5. I'm thinking of a word that ends with K.
It has five letters.
It rhymes with **take**.
You have to do this to an egg when you open it.
(Answer: *break*)

6. I'm thinking of a word that ends with E.
It has three letters.
It's a wonderful dessert.
Sometimes you make it with apples.
(Answer: *pie*)

7. I'm thinking of a word that ends with N.
It has four letters.
It rhymes with **pin**.
If you eat too much you will never be _____.
(Answer: *thin*)

1.			C	H	E	E	S	E
2.			H	U	N	G	R	Y
3.			I	C	E			
4.			C	R	E	A	M	
5.	B	R	E	A	K			
6.			P	I	E			
7.		T	H	I	N			

UNIT 10

Exercise 1

1. It *costs a* lot *to* live *in the* city.
2. *How* much *does it* cost?
3. *It* costs *an awful* lot.
4. Why *don't* you *buy it*?
5. *It's* too *expensive*. I *can't* afford *it*.

Exercise 2

1. It costs a lot to eat out these days.
2. It's not worth it.
3. I can't believe how much it costs.
4. I'll get it this time.
5. You got it last time.

Exercise 3

1. I'm thinking of a word that starts with M.
   It has five letters.
   You need it to live well.
   They say it cannot bring happiness.
   (Answer: *money*)

2. I'm thinking of a word that starts with O.
   It has three letters.
   It rhymes with **cough**.
   It's the opposite of **on**.
   (Answer: *off*)

3. I'm thinking of a word that starts with N.
   It has five letters.
   It rhymes with **clever**.
   It's the opposite of **always**.
   (Answer: *never*)

4. I'm thinking of a word that starts with E.
   It has four letters.
   It has two syllables.
   It's the opposite of **difficult**.
   (Answer: *easy*)

5. I'm thinking of a word that starts with Y.
   It has four letters.
   It has 365 days.
   It rhymes with **here**.
   (Answer: *year*)

Answer Key

1. M	O	N	E	Y
2. O	F	F		
3. N	E	V	E	R
4. E	A	S	Y	
5. Y	E	A	R	

UNIT 11

Exercise 1

1. *It's a* nice *day* today, *isn't* it?
2. It *certainly* is. It's *a* beautiful *day*.
3. It's *too* hot *to* walk *to* work *today*.
4. *It's* much *too* hot, *hot* and *humid*.
5. Look *at* the *sky*. It's clear *as a* bell.
6. Do *you* think *it's* going *to* rain?
7. Put *on* your *sweater*. It's bitter *cold*.
8. *Wear* something *warm*. *It's* cold *outside*.
9. *It's* freezing. Do *you* think *it's* going *to* snow?
10. I *hope* not.

Exercise 2

1. It's cold outside. It's bitter cold.
2. It's freezing. Wear something warm.
3. Do you think it's going to rain?
4. It's too hot to walk to work.
5. It's a beautiful day today, isn't it?

Exercise 3

1. I'm thinking of a word that starts with W.
   It has four letters.
   It's nice to feel like this on a cold night.
   It's the opposite of **cool**.
   (Answer: *warm*)

2. I'm thinking of a word that ends with E.
   It has six letters.
   It rhymes with **please**.
   It happens to water in the winter.
   (Answer: *freeze*)

3. I'm thinking of a word that starts with A.
   It has six letters.
   It has two syllables.
   It's the opposite of **never**.
   (Answer: *always*)

4. I'm thinking of a word that starts with T.
   It has three letters.
   It tastes good on a cold day.
   It's something you drink.
   (Answer: *tea*)

5. I'm thinking of a word that starts with H.
   It has three letters.
   It sounds like **not**.
   It's the opposite of **cold**.
   (Answer: *hot*)

6. I'm thinking of a word that starts with E.
   It has three letters.
   It rhymes with **feet**.
   Many people do this three times a day.
   (Answer: *eat*)

7. I'm thinking of a word that starts with R.
   It has four letters.
   It spoils picnics.
   It rhymes with **pain**.
   (Answer: *rain*)

Answer Key

```
1.                    W   A   R   M
2.  F   R   E   E   Z   E
3.                    A   L   W   A   Y   S
4.                    T   E   A
5.                    H   O   T
6.                    E   A   T
7.                    R   A   I   N
```

UNIT 12

Exercise 1

1. *How* long *does it* take?
2. It *takes a* long *time*.
3. Does *this* bus *go* downtown?
4. Is *there* a *newspaper* stand *near* here?
5. Yes, *there is*. *Walk* two *blocks* and *turn* left.
6. *Is* the *post office* open *tomorrow*?
7. *It's* open *from* nine *to* five.
8. When *does* it *open*?
9. It *opens* at *nine*.
10. *Are* the *stores* open *tomorrow*?

Exercise 2

1. Are the stores open tomorrow?
2. Is there a coffee shop near here?
3. Yes, there is. Walk two blocks and turn left.
4. How long does it take?
5. It takes three and a half months.

Exercise 3

1. I'm thinking of a word that starts with W.
   It has three letters.
   It's a question word.
   It rhymes with **my**.
   (Answer: *why*)

2. I'm thinking of a word that starts with H.
   It has three letters.
   It's used to ask a question.
   It rhymes with **now**.
   (Answer: *how*)

3. I'm thinking of a word that has four letters.
   The third letter is E.
   It's a question word.
   It rhymes with **ten**.
   (Answer: *when*)

4. I'm thinking of a word that has five letters.
   The fourth letter is R.
   It's a question word.
   It rhymes with **hair**.
   (Answer: *where*)

5. I'm thinking of a word that has five letters.
   It ends with E.
   It rhymes with **me**.
   It's the answer to the question, "What's a crowd?"
   (Answer: *three*)

Answer Key

```
1.                    W   H   Y
2.                    H   O   W
3.            W   H   E   N
4.        W   H   E   R   E
5.  T   H   R   E   E
```

Exercise 4

It takes six hours to fly to San Francisco from New York. There is a three-hour time difference between the East Coast and the West Coast. The East Coast is three hours AHEAD of the West Coast.

Answer Key

1. 3 A.M.
2. 6:45 A.M.

UNIT 13

Exercise 1

1. *Thank* you *so* much. *It's* just *what* I *wanted*.
2. I'm *glad* you *like* it.
3. *That* was *very* nice *of* you.
4. *I'm* glad I *was* able *to* help.
5. Thanks *again*. I *appreciate* it.
6. Don't *mention* it. It *was* my *pleasure*.
7. You *shouldn't* have *done* it.
8. I *wanted* to. The *pleasure* was *mine*.

Exercise 2

1. Thanks a lot for everything.
2. You shouldn't have done it.
3. That was awfully nice of you.
4. I'm so glad you like it.
5. It's just the right color.

Exercise 4

1. I'm thinking of a word that starts with T.
   It has five letters.
   It rhymes with **rough**.
   It's the opposite of **tender**.
   It's difficult to eat a _____ steak.
   (Answer: *tough*)

2. I'm thinking of a word that starts with H.
   It has five letters.
   It has two syllables.
   It's the opposite of **sad**.
   (Answer: *happy*)

3. I'm thinking of a word that starts with A.
   It has five letters.
   It has two syllables.
   It's the opposite of **before**.
   (Answer: *after*)

4. I'm thinking of a word that starts with N.
   It has four letters.
   It rhymes with **rice**.
   It's the opposite of **nasty**.
   (Answer: *nice*)

5. I'm thinking of a word that starts with K.
It has four letters.
It rhymes with **steep**.
It ends with P.
Some people can't _____ a secret.
(Answer: *keep*)

6. I'm thinking of a word that starts with S.
It has eight letters.
It ends with E.
It has two syllables
It's something you do not expect.
(Answer: *surprise*)

Answer Key

1. **T** O U G H
2. **H** A P P Y
3. **A** F T E R
4. **N** I C E
5. **K** E E P
6. **S** U R P R I S E

UNIT 14

Exercise 1

1. *This* is *confusing*. I *can't* understand *what* he's *saying*, can *you*?
2. No, I *can't*. He's *talking* too *quickly*.
3. *I'm* very *confused*. I *can't* understand *him*.
4. I'm *totally* lost.
5. *So* am *I*. I'm *all* mixed *up*.
6. *Where's* the *hotel*? *Where* do *we* go?
7. *I'm* not *quite* sure *just* where *we* are.
8. What *shall* we *do*?
9. *Don't* ask *me*. I *was* counting *on* you.
10. I *thought* you *knew*.

Exercise 2

1. This is confusing. I can't understand him.
2. I thought you had the tickets.
3. I can't figure it out, can you?
4. I'm not quite sure just where we are.
5. What are we supposed to do?

Exercise 3

1. Jack bought 13 books. They cost $30 apiece. How much did he spend?
2. Aunt Alice is 80 years old. Her sister Jane is four years younger than she is. How old is Jane?
3. Mr. and Mrs. Brown went to Florida on Thursday the 13th of June. They stayed ten days. When did they arrive home?
4. Bill came to New York when he was five years old. He has lived there for 18 years. How old is he now?
5. Jim is four years older than his brother and two years older than his sister. If his sister is 13, how old is Jim's brother?

1. $390
2. 76 years old
3. June 23rd
4. 23 years old
5. 11 years old

UNIT 15

Exercise 1

1. What *are you going to* do *when* you finish *this* course?
2. *I'm* not *quite* sure. What *are you* going *to* do?
3. I *haven't* decided. What *about* you?
4. *It* all *depends*.
5. *Can* we get *together* tomorrow *at* three?
6. I'm *sorry,* that's *a* little *too* early *for* me. How *about* eight?
7. *That's* a *little* too *late*.
8. *I'd* love *to* see *you*. *When* are you *free*?
9. *Call* me *tomorrow*. I *finish* at *three*. *Is* three *OK*?
10. *Whatever* you *say* is *fine* with *me*.

Exercise 2

1. Let's make a date.
2. I'd love to see you.
3. Can we get together tomorrow at three?
4. I've got so much to do I don't know what to do first.
5. What'll you do if it doesn't go well?

Exercise 3

A Go shopping
Cash a check
Go to the bank
B Invite ten friends for dinner
Look at your date book
Check your financial situation
C Go to the supermarket
See what's in your refrigerator
Make a shopping list
D Get married
Look for a good job
Have a few kids